Katie Can't Eat Nuts

The Ordinary Extraordinary Life of a Girl with Food Allergies

Written By

KATHERINE A. KISE

Illustrated By

ALEX FERROR

Kise, Katherine A. *Katie Can't Eat Nuts:*
The Ordinary Extraordinary Life of a Girl with Food Allergies

Copyright © 2021 by Katherine A. Kise
Written by Katherine A. Kise
Illustrated by Alex Ferror
Layout design and logo by Liona Design Co.
Published by KWE Publishing: www.kwepub.com All rights reserved.

ISBN (hardback) 978-1-950306-31-2
ISBN (ebook) 978-1-950306-32-9

Library of Congress Control Number: 2021907162

KWE Publishing LLC.
www.kwepub.com

To Mom and Dad,

for your unwavering support, loving foundation, and steadfast belief in me and my dreams — no matter what!

And also to Mary Beth,

for being the best big sister I could ever ask for ♥

Hi, I'm Katie! I go to elementary school, and I love
to play soccer with my friends.

I'm also a ballerina, and on Saturdays, I make
pancakes with my dad and go to the park!

And, I also have food allergies.

I can't eat any foods that have nuts.

Sometimes, if I eat something I'm not supposed to eat,
I can get really sick. So I avoid foods that have nuts in them.

Once, when I was at a party, I ate a cookie that had nuts in it. I got very sick, and couldn't breathe. It was really scary. When my mom took me to the doctor, he told me that I was allergic to nuts, and I have to be careful with what I eat.

Look at everything else I CAN eat!

So, it's ok that I can't have those other things!

My dad makes my sandwiches with other butters and spreads,
like tahini and sunflower seed butter! They're so good!

When I think I might have eaten something I'm allergic to, I get scared,
and sometimes I feel different than other kids. Feeling different can be hard.

My parents, teachers, and friends look out for me so that
I don't eat anything that might make me sick.

Some of my friends even make special treats,
so we can enjoy eating snacks together!

My friend George is allergic to gluten, so we
are really careful with him at school, too.

Some kids are allergic to bees, too! We look out for each other on the playground, so we can all stay safe!

I learned in school that millions of kids have food allergies! That's more than 1,000 times the number of stars we can see in the sky!

Even if sometimes I feel different, I know I'm not alone. Lots of kids are learning how to figure out food allergies!

Being different is ok. My mom says every kid is unique, which is what makes each of us so special! Having friends who aren't exactly alike is more fun!

Speaking of friends and fun, I see George
and Elsa on the see-saw! Bye for now!

ACTIVITIES
SECTION

KATIE'S WORLD WORD SEARCH

R	E	P	Y	L	P	E	B	P	I	C	K	L	E
T	O	C	I	R	P	A	S	A	E	K	P	E	A
A	L	L	E	R	G	Y	N	E	N	P	M	L	H
R	R	M	K	R	A	P	N	C	N	A	M	Y	S
S	B	A	L	L	E	R	I	N	A	O	N	D	G
O	L	E	P	A	G	N	N	Y	N	K	N	A	A
C	C	C	E	K	P	A	P	D	C	E	E	A	R
C	N	I	T	R	T	P	E	N	I	K	P	S	P
E	R	U	A	A	T	C	L	R	N	E	E	O	E
R	U	J	R	R	R	G	F	E	A	P	L	E	L
I	N	L	A	P	E	A	N	U	T	K	L	I	M
C	Y	O	K	F	E	I	E	A	Z	Z	I	P	S
T	N	C	H	O	C	O	L	A	T	E	C	E	O
R	N	Y	P	U	L	K	A	I	M	E	I	C	L

BALLERINA
PANCAKES
SOCCER
PARK
FRIENDS
PIZZA
APPLE
PEANUT
ALMOND
CHOCOLATE
BANANA
APRICOT
PICKLE
KARATE
MILK
GYM
JUICE
TREE
RUN
ALLERGY

24

Katie loves her ballet classes, but she can't find a matching pair
of ballet slippers! Can you help her find the matching pairs?

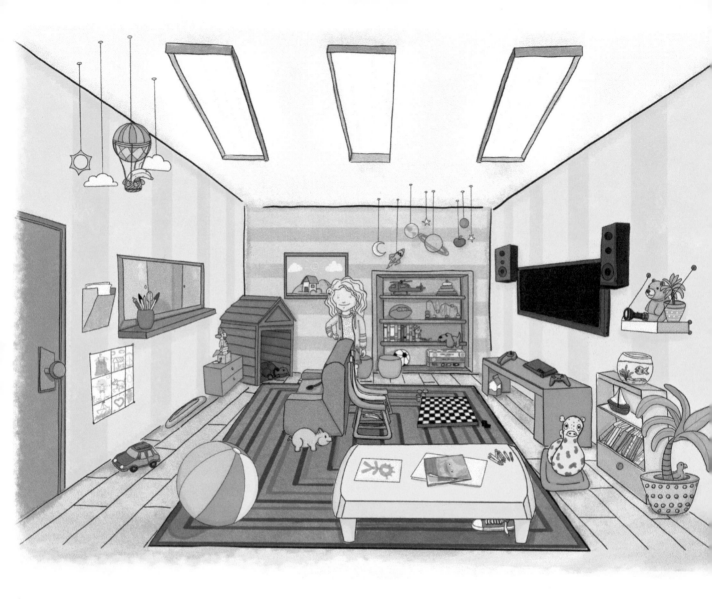

The doctor's office is full of surprises! Can you find
the hidden items at Katie's doctor's office? Look for:

1. A banana   2. A sailboat   3. A leaf   4. An apple
5. A shoe   6. A flashlight   7. A soccer ball 8. A milk carton

Katie loves to play, but she can't find a matching pair of socks!
Can you help her find the matching pairs? Do you match your socks?

RIDDLES

1. What has a face and two hands, but no arms or legs?

2. What has to be broken before you can use it?

3. What comes out at night without being called,
    and is lost in the day without being stolen?

4. What is easy to get into, but hard to get out of?

5. What gets sharper the more you use it?

6. What is full of keys but can't open any door?

7. What kind of coat can only be put on when wet?

8. What follows you and copies your every move,
    but you can't touch it or catch it?

9. What building has thousands of stories?

10. What are two things you can NEVER
    eat for breakfast?

1. A clock 2. An egg 3. A star 4. Trouble 5. Your brain 6. A piano 7. A coat of paint 8. Your shadow 9. The library 10. Lunch and dinner

Do you like pancakes? Katie makes pancakes with her dad on Saturdays. Decorate these pancakes with your favorite toppings!

What fun the playground can be! Can you find the items hidden on Katie and George's school playground? Look for:

1. A spatula
2. A bowl
3. A pencil
4. A lollipop
5. A bunch of grapes
6. A baseball cap
7. A bird
8. A kite
9. A pacifier
10. A football
11. A pearl necklace
12. A kitten

There are so many stars in the sky; what do you see?
Do you wish upon stars? What do you wish for?

PUZZLE
SOLUTIONS

KATIE'S WORLD WORD SEARCH

R	E	P	Y	L	P	E	B	P	I	C	K	L	E	BALLERINA
T	O	C	I	R	P	A	S	A	E	K	P	E	A	PANCAKES
A	L	L	E	R	G	Y	N	E	N	P	M	L	H	SOCCER
R	R	M	K	R	A	P	N	C	N	A	M	Y	S	PARK
S	B	A	L	L	E	R	I	N	A	O	N	D	G	FRIENDS
O	L	E	P	A	G	N	N	Y	N	K	N	A	A	PIZZA
C	C	C	E	K	P	A	P	D	C	E	E	A	R	APPLE
C	N	I	T	R	T	P	E	N	I	K	P	S	P	PEANUT
E	R	U	A	A	T	C	L	R	N	E	E	O	E	ALMOND
R	U	J	R	R	R	G	F	E	A	P	L	E	L	CHOCOLATE
I	N	L	A	P	E	A	N	U	T	K	L	I	M	BANANA
C	Y	O	K	F	E	I	E	A	Z	Z	I	P	S	APRICOT
T	N	C	H	O	C	O	L	A	T	E	C	E	O	PICKLE
R	N	Y	P	U	L	K	A	I	M	E	I	C	L	KARATE

BALLERINA
PANCAKES
SOCCER
PARK
FRIENDS
PIZZA
APPLE
PEANUT
ALMOND
CHOCOLATE
BANANA
APRICOT
PICKLE
KARATE
MILK
GYM
JUICE
TREE
RUN
ALLERGY

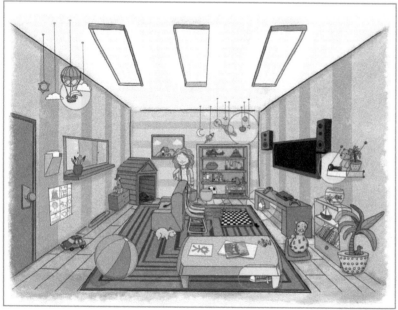

37

ABOUT THE AUTHOR
KATHERINE A. KISE

Self-proclaimed "wellness junkie" **Katherine A. Kise** suffered from a severe nut allergy and asthma as a child. As an adult, she developed additional allergies, auto-immune imbalances, and chronic illnesses, despite a "healthy" and active lifestyle. Katherine began building a knowledge base of holistic health practices and resources that eventually helped her uncover the underlying causes of her health issues and overcome them. Now as a board certified health coach, Katherine helps others navigate their own health concerns. Her first book, *Katie Can't Eat Nuts*, is a story that follows a young girl's extraordinary life, revealing a strong and feisty girl who plays soccer, takes ballet, and happens to be allergic to nuts. Uplifting, informative, and spirited, Katie's story helps children with allergies feel accepted and confident.

ABOUT THE ILLUSTRATOR
ALEX FERROR

Alex Ferror is a Brazilian self-taught illustrator, muralist, and fine artist based in Lisbon, Portugal. Alex describes himself as a visual storyteller and his art as whimsical allegories for our daily lives. In his colorful work, Alex invites you to connect with your inner child. The artist explores the whimsical universe of children's imagination and how kids see the world and interact with their feelings. Through his characters, mostly children and their imaginary friends, Alex encourages diversity, creativity, love, and respect, among other messages and emotions that the artist considers essential since childhood. Although Alex's work can be seen on walls, installations, publications, and products in different countries, *Katie Can't Eat Nuts*, originally published in 2021, is his first illustrated children's book.

CPSIA information can be obtained
at www.ICGtesting.com
Printed in the USA
LVHW070138110621
689904LV00003B/112